In the spotlight

A NIACE briefing on participation in learning by adults from minority ethnic groups

Fiona Aldridge, Yanina Dutton and Alan Tuckett

EUROPEAN UNION
European Social Fund

Local Government Association

promoting adult learning

Published by the National Institute of Adult Continuing Education
(England and Wales)

21 De Montfort Street
Leicester LE1 7GE
Company registration no. 2603322
Charity registration no. 1002775

The production of this publication has been part-funded by the European
Social Fund in association with Adult Learners' Week 2006.
The European Social Fund is a European Union initiative that supports
activities to promote employment opportunities for all. Visit the website at
www.esf.gov.uk

EUROPEAN UNION
European Social Fund

NIACE, the national organisation for adult learning, has a broad remit to
promote lifelong learning opportunities for adults. NIACE works to develop increased participation in education and training, particularly for those
who do not have easy access because of barriers of class, gender, age, race,
language and culture, learning difficulties and disabilities, or insufficient
financial resources.

NIACE's website on the internet is **http://www.niace.org.uk**

Cataloguing in Publication Data
A CIP record of this title is available from the British Library

ISBN 1 86201 294 6
      978 1 86201 294 3

ii

Contents

Acknowledgements

We are grateful for the support of the European Social Fund and the Local Government Association in the funding of this work; and of our colleagues at NIACE in the production of this report

Introduction

Every year the National Institute of Adult Continuing Education undertakes a representative sample survey of about 5,000 adults in the UK population, to map adult participation in learning, and to identify those groups relatively under-represented in learning.[1] Over time these surveys show the persistence of the influence of social class, age, prior educational experience, and employment status on people's willingness to participate. For too many people, the perception lingers that 'education's for other people'. The rest of NIACE's work shows that there is nothing inevitable about the marginalisation of under-represented groups – but that there needs to be sustained and focused work by educators to widen participation and achievement successfully.

The size of the annual survey sample precludes NIACE from disaggregating overall findings for distinct minority ethnic groups, so in 1992 Naomi Sargant undertook a dedicated survey[2] for the Institute, and in 2003 we published *Light and Shade*,[3] the results of analysing ethnic minority group participation, using the much larger samples of the government's Labour Force Survey. This report follows on from that one – drawing on the most recently available public data, from 2004.

NIACE is aware of the difficulty of using ethnic descriptors such as 'Pakistani'. Such terms may encompass second- or third-generation British citizens whose forbears arrived from Pakistan as well as more recent arrivals. The terms used are those self-identified by survey participants when asked about ethnic background. It is not our intention to reinforce exclusion, or 'otherness', in reporting survey results.

The findings of *In the Spotlight* are stark. Whilst the participation rate of ethnic minority groups as a whole is within a single percentage point of the UK population's it is five percentage points down when account is taken of the different age profile of Britain's black and minority ethnic communities. That leaves room for sustained activity to ensure that all Britain's communities can benefit from the Government's commitment to securing economic prosperity and social cohesion through lifelong learning.

However, it is the different experience of different groups that is the sharpest finding overall. Adults from Bangladeshi and Pakistani communities fare dramatically worse than all other groups. Participation overall among Bangladeshi adults is just 40 per cent, against 64 per cent for the adult population overall. Just 29 per cent of Bangladeshi adults have a Level 2 qualification or better – the equivalent of five good GCSEs, against 60 per cent for the adult population

1 This year's report, *Green Shoots?*, will be published by NIACE during Adult Learners' Week, May 20–26 2006.
2 Sargant, N. (1993) *Learning for a purpose: participation in education and training by adults from ethnic minorities*, NIACE: Leicester.
3 Aldridge, F. and Tuckett, A. (2003) *Light and Shade: A NIACE briefing on participation in adult learning by adults from minority ethnic groups*, NIACE: Leicester.

overall. Forty-three per cent of Bangladeshi community adults have no qualifications at all – against 32 per cent for adults of Pakistani origin, and 17 per cent in the overall adult population. Yet when Bangladeshi adults do get a Level 2 qualification their participation rates soar. At work, just 7 per cent of Bangladeshi adults report having trained in the last 4 weeks, against 25 per cent overall, but Bangladeshi and Pakistani adults in work are much more likely to learn than those outside it. And among those Bangladeshi and Pakistani adults who are engaged in learning there is a far higher incidence of self-organised as distinct from taught learning. The size of the gap between Bangladeshi and Pakistani adults and all the other groups surveyed highlights the social exclusion of these communities. There are key messages for schools here – the longer learners from these communities stay in the system, and the more they achieve, the more likely they are to engage in learning later on. And for post-school education, the challenges are equally powerful. Shortages in provision of English for Speakers of Other Languages, and the absence of coherent foundation- level studies, starting from the experience and aspirations of the learners, perpetuate marginalisation and need to be addressed.

Once again, in the question posed about faith affiliation, it is Muslim adults who are dramatically less likely to participate than others with different faith affiliations. Given the findings of the Research Centre for the Wider Benefits of Learning at the University of London's Institute of Education that participation in learning increases respect for diversity and intercommunal understanding,[4] no policy maker can be relaxed about the results reported here.

For other minority ethnic communities the picture is a more optimistic one – for some, like Black African adults, and mixed-race adults, there is evidence of participation levels that exceed the population overall, for others engagement is broadly similar. There can be no room for complacency anywhere, however, when, as Lord Leitch's interim report on the skills needs of the UK in 2020[5] suggests, skill levels across the population need to rise everywhere. Nevertheless, the key finding of this report is that the extent of under-participation by Bangladeshi and Pakistani adults presents a major challenge to the education and training system, and to employers alike.

---

4 Preston, J. and Feinstein, L. (2004) *Adult education and attitude change (Research report no.11)*, Centre for Research on the Wider Benefits of Learning: London.
5 Leitch Review of Skills (2005) *Skills in the UK: The Long Term Challenge – Interim Report*, TSO, London

Technical notes

This NIACE briefing on participation in adult learning by adults from minority ethnic groups is mainly based upon data from the 2004 ONS Labour Force Survey. The Labour Force Survey (LFS) is a quarterly sample survey of households living at private addresses in Great Britain. Its purpose is to provide information on the UK labour market that can then be used to develop, manage, evaluate and report on labour market policies. The questionnaire design, sample selection, and interviewing are carried out by the Social and Vital Statistics Division of the Office for National Statistics (ONS) on behalf of the Statistical Outputs Group of the ONS.

• All tables within this briefing are rounded to the nearest whole percentage point.

• All tables are percentaged vertically unless otherwise specified.

• In tables, * indicates less than 0.5 per cent but greater than zero, and – indicates zero. NSR indicates not separately recorded and NA indicates not asked.

Participation in learning

The 2004 ONS Labour Force Survey shows that when taken together, adults from minority ethnic groups participate in learning at a similar level (63 per cent) to that of the adult population in general (64 per cent).

These overall figures, however, mask marked differences between different minority ethnic groups (see Table 1). Black Africans (77 per cent), adults of mixed ethnic origin (76 per cent), Chinese (68 per cent), and adults from *other* minority ethnic groups (68 per cent) exhibit higher than average levels of participation in learning, while Pakistani (48 per cent) and Bangladeshi (40 per cent) adults are much less likely to participate in learning. Respondents of Black Caribbean (65 per cent) and Indian (63 per cent) origin were found to participate at a level similar to that of the adult population as a whole.

In order to take account of the younger age profile of minority ethnic groups, Table 1 also shows participation in learning by adults of working age. Among this group, levels of participation in learning for adults from minority ethnic groups (67 per cent) are slightly lower than those for all respondents (72 per cent).

Analysis of these data by ethnicity also shows similar differences between minority ethnic groups. Black Africans (78 per cent) and adults of mixed ethnic origin (78 per cent) again are found to be more likely to participate in learning, as are Black Caribbeans (73 per cent). Participation levels for Pakistani (50 per cent) and Bangladeshi (43 per cent) adults of working age are once more at below average.

Table 1. Participation in learning by ethnicity

	All adults %	All adults of working age %
All respondents	64	72
All adults from minority ethnic groups	63	67
Black African	77	78
Black Caribbean	65	73
Chinese	68	71
Indian	63	68
Pakistani	48	50
Bangladeshi	40	43
Mixed ethnic origin	76	78
Other	68	71

Source: *ONS Labour Force Survey, UK*, 2004

Type of learning

When asked about the type of learning that they were involved in 70 per cent of all learners said that they were involved in some form of taught learning, with 30 per cent participating only in self-directed learning. In comparison, around three-quarters of ethnic minority adult learners (74 per cent) were engaged in taught learning, with one-quarter (26 per cent) engaged only in self-directed learning (see Table 2).

Pakistani (33 per cent) and Bangladeshi learners (34 per cent) are more likely than other groups of minority ethnic adult learners to engage only in self-directed learning. That is, although they are learning, they are not engaging with the education and training system. In contrast, Black Africans (82 per cent) in particular are more likely to be engaged in taught learning.

Table 2: Type of learning, by ethnicity

	Taught learning[6] %	Self-directed learning only %
All respondents	70	30
All minority ethnic groups	74	26
Black African	82	18
Black Caribbean	76	24
Chinese	71	29
Indian	72	28
Pakistani	67	33
Bangladeshi	66	34
Mixed ethnic origin	79	22
Other	75	25

Base: all adults who have participated in learning during the previous 12 months
Source: *ONS Labour Force Survey, UK*, 2004

---

6 Includes taught learning only as well as taught and self-directed learning.

Learning and qualifications

Seventeen per cent of the general adult population of working age and 20 per cent of the minority ethnic adult population of working age in the UK do not possess any qualifications. In particular, a high proportion of Pakistani (32 per cent) and Bangladeshi (43 per cent) adults have no qualifications.

Around one-quarter of all adults from minority ethnic groups have a qualification at Level 4 or above, 12 per cent are qualified at Level 3, 11 per cent at Level 2 and 10 per cent below Level 2. For one in five ethnic minority adults, their highest level of qualification lies outside of the National Qualifications Framework. These qualifications have often been gained overseas and may not be recognised within the UK.

Three-fifths of the general adult population of working age and around half (49 per cent) of the minority ethnic population of working age in the UK are qualified to at least Level 2. Adults of mixed ethnic origin (63 per cent) are most likely to have a Level 2 qualification, while only 29 per cent of Bangladeshis, 40 per cent of Pakistanis and 42 per cent of adults from *other* minority ethnic groups are qualified to this level.

Table 3: Highest level of qualification, by ethnicity

	NVQ Level 4 and above %	NVQ Level 3 %	NVQ Level 2 %	Level 2 and above %	Below NVQ Level 2 %	Other qualifications %	No qualifications %
All respondents	28	16	16	60	15	9	17
All minority ethnic groups	26	12	11	49	10	20	20
Black African	30	12	12	54	8	24	15
Black Caribbean	23	14	19	56	21	9	14
Chinese	35	9	8	52	5	25	18
Indian	32	14	10	56	8	20	16
Pakistani	16	11	13	40	12	16	32
Bangladeshi	10	10	9	29	11	17	43
Mixed ethnic origin	27	18	18	63	14	10	13
Other	27	8	7	42	6	31	20

Base: all adults of working age (excludes trade apprentices)

Source: *ONS Labour Force Survey, UK*, 2004

Participation in learning by highest level of qualification

The proposed entitlement for learning up to a first Level 3 qualification for those aged 19–30, and up to a first Level 2 qualification for those aged 19 and over, is based on the presumption that after this, employers and individuals can both see the benefit of continued investment in learning.

Table 4 below shows levels of participation in learning among different minority ethnic groups by the highest level of qualification held. Across all groups, adults with higher levels of qualification are more likely to participate in learning than those with lower levels of, or no, qualifications. Nearly nine in ten adults from minority ethnic groups with a Level 4 qualification report participation in learning, compared with 82 per cent of those with a highest qualification at level 3, 74 per cent of those with a highest qualification at Level 2, 66 per cent of those with a qualification below Level 2 and 36 per cent of those without any qualifications at all.

Table 4 suggests that for most adults from minority ethnic groups, gaining any qualification at all is the key trigger in increasing rates of participation. It also provides some support for government in revealing that the achievement of a Level 2 qualification is a highly significant trigger for increased participation in learning for Chinese, Bangladeshi and 'other' ethnic minority ethnic groups, but has a negligible impact among participation among Black Caribbean's and adults of mixed ethnic origin.

Finally, the achievement of a Level 4 qualification is also a key trigger for increased participation in learning, particularly for Bangladeshi, Pakistani and 'other' minority ethnic groups.

Table 4: Participation in learning, by highest level of qualification, by ethnicity

	All adults of working age %	NVQ Level 4 and above %	NVQ Level 3 %	NVQ Level 2 %	Below NVQ Level 2 %	Other qualifications %	No qualifications %
All respondents	73	91	82	78	68	68	40
All minority ethnic groups	68	88	78	74	66	67	36
Black African	78	90	85	86	80	72	54
Black Caribbean	74	87	84	76	75	71	43
Chinese	71	84	83	63	46	80	44
Indian	69	89	80	71	62	65	32
Pakistani	50	85	69	64	55	48	23
Bangladeshi	44	88	57	62	52	58	23
Mixed ethnic origin	78	89	80	77	79	79	51
Other	71	88	76	82	63	73	45

Base: all adults of working age
Source: *ONS Labour Force Survey, UK*, 2004

Learning for a qualification

Adult learners from minority ethnic groups (19 per cent) are more likely to be working towards a qualification than learners within the general adult population (15 per cent). In particular, Black African learners (28 per cent), and learners of mixed ethnic origin (24 per cent) are most likely to be working towards a qualification (see Table 5).

Table 5: Proportion of learners working towards a qualification, by ethnicity

	All learners of working age in employment %
All respondents	15
All minority ethnic groups	19
Black African	28
Black Caribbean	18
Chinese	21
Indian	15
Pakistani	16
Bangladeshi	14
Mixed ethnic origin	24
Other	19

Base: all learners of working age in employment

Source: *ONS Labour Force Survey, UK,* 2004

Participation in job-related education and training

Thirty-one per cent of both the general adult population and of the minority ethnic adult population, of working age in employment, reported participation in job-related education and training in the 13 weeks prior to the survey interview taking place.

Again, however, these opportunities are not equally distributed (see Table 6). It is encouraging that 43 per cent of Black Africans and 40 per cent of adults of mixed ethnic origin in work were offered opportunities to engage in job-related education and training. In contrast, however, only around one-quarter of Chinese (25 per cent) and Pakistani (23 per cent) adults in work, and fewer than one in five Bangladeshi adults (18 per cent) in work also received access to such opportunities.

Table 6: Participation in job-related training and education in the past 13 weeks, by ethnicity

	All adults of working age in employment %
All respondents	31
All minority ethnic groups	31
Black African	43
Black Caribbean	31
Chinese	25
Indian	29
Pakistani	23
Bangladeshi	18
Mixed ethnic origin	40
Other	32

Base: all adults of working age in employment
Source: *ONS Labour Force Survey, UK*, 2004

A similar pattern occurs in relation to participation in job-related education and training in the 4 weeks prior to the survey interview taking place, with around one in six of both all adults (16 per cent) and all adults from minority ethnic groups (17 per cent) of working age in employment participating (see Table 7).

Again, Black Africans were most likely to receive opportunities to engage in job-related education and training (25 per cent), while only 7 per cent of Bangladeshi adults in employment received such opportunities.

Table 7: Participation in job-related training and education in the past 4 weeks, by ethnicity

	All adults of working age in employment %
All respondents	16
All minority ethnic groups	17
Black African	25
Black Caribbean	16
Chinese	15
Indian	14
Pakistani	14
Bangladeshi	7
Mixed ethnic origin	22
Other	18

Base: all adults of working age in employment
Source: *ONS Labour Force Survey, UK*, 2004

Participation in learning – demographic analysis

Participation in learning by gender

The survey shows that within the general adult population, a higher proportion of men (67 per cent) rather than women (60 per cent) are participating in learning. This pattern is also replicated within the minority ethnic population, although with a smaller gender difference than among the general adult population (see Table 8).

Again, there are marked differences between groups: Pakistani and Bangladeshi men in particular are much more likely than their female counterparts to be learning, although men from both groups are still less likely to participate than men from any other minority ethnic group. In contrast, women of Caribbean background are more likely then men to be learning.

Table 8: Participation in learning by gender, by ethnicity

	All %	Men %	Women %
All respondents	64	67	60
All minority ethnic groups	63	65	62
Black African	77	80	74
Black Caribbean	65	62	67
Chinese	68	69	67
Indian	63	66	60
Pakistani	48	52	43
Bangladeshi	40	47	33
Mixed ethnic origin	76	77	75
Other	68	70	67

Base: all adults
Source: *ONS Labour Force Survey, UK*, 2004

Participation in learning by age

Among both the adult population in general, and the minority ethnic population in particular, participation in learning generally declines with age, with those under 30 much less likely to be learning than those aged 30 and over (see Table 9).

Among Black Africans, Black Caribbeans, adults of mixed ethnic origin and 'other' adults from minority ethnic groups there is a gentle decline in participation among adults of working age. Pakistani and Bangladeshi adults, however, not only start with lower levels of participation among young adults, but also experience a much more severe decline in participation among the working age population.

The decline in participation is particularly steep for those adults aged 55 and over. Participation levels for older Black Africans remain relatively high (47 per cent of those aged 65 and over). In comparison, only 4 per cent of Bangladeshi adults in this age group report participation in learning.

The difference in participation rates between those aged under 30 and those aged 30 and over are smallest for Black Africans and adults of mixed ethnic origin and greatest for adults of Bangladeshi, Pakistani and Indian origin.

Table 9: Participation in learning by age, by ethnicity

	All %	Under 30 %	30 and over %	16–24 %	25–34 %	35–44 %	45–54 %	55–64 %	65+ %
All respondents	64	78	60	78	77	75	72	58	29
All minority ethnic groups	63	74	60	75	72	68	59	50	22
Black African	77	82	75	79	84	75	77	61	47
Black Caribbean	65	75	62	77	75	76	73	55	24
Chinese	68	80	63	84	78	73	62	42	18
Indian	63	79	58	81	79	70	54	50	20
Pakistani	48	61	42	63	57	46	35	27	15
Bangladeshi	40	56	32	62	45	41	29	18	4
Mixed ethnic origin	76	79	73	80	78	78	79	67	30
Other	68	76	66	76	74	71	66	59	29

Base: all adults
Source: *ONS Labour Force Survey, UK*, 2004

Participation in learning by economic activity

Among the general adult population, those in employment (81 per cent) are more likely to be learning then those who are unemployed (66 per cent), with both groups being considerably more likely to be learners than adults who are inactive (35 per cent). Within the minority ethnic population, the pattern is very similar (see Table 10) although there are slightly higher levels of participation among inactive adults (40 per cent), and slightly lower levels of participation among those in employment (78 per cent).

Across all categories of economic activity, Pakistani and Bangladeshi adults are least likely to be learning. Among those who are inactive, Indian adults are also less likely than other groups to be learners. The greatest differences in participation rates between those in employment and the unemployed are seen among Caribbean and Bangladeshi adults.

Table 10: Participation in learning by economic activity, by ethnicity

	All %	In employment %	Unemployed[7] %	Inactive %
All respondents	64	81	66	35
All minority ethnic groups	63	78	67	40
Black African	77	87	75	60
Black Caribbean	65	81	64	38
Chinese	68	76	67	53
Indian	63	76	69	34
Pakistani	48	66	59	29
Bangladeshi	40	64	49	21
Mixed ethnic origin	76	85	75	53
Other	68	80	70	50

Base: all adults
Source: *ONS Labour Force Survey, UK*, 2004

7. Includes only those who are registered as unemployed and claiming Job Seeker's Allowance.

Participation in learning by socio-economic classification

Within both the general adult population and the minority ethnic population, participation levels in higher socio-economic classes are greater than those in lower classes (see Table 11). Nine in ten of adults from minority ethnic groups in managerial and professional occupations are learning compared with 73 per cent in intermediate occupations and 66 per cent in routine and manual occupations.

Within each of the categories in the table below, there is a greater drop in participation between managerial & professional occupations and intermediate occupations, than between intermediate and routine & manual occupations. The greatest drop in participation between the highest and lowest classes is seen among Indian, Pakistani and Bangladeshi adults.

Table 11: Participation in learning by socio-economic classification, by ethnicity

	Managerial & professional occupations %	Intermediate occupations %	All in employment %	Routine & manual occupations %
All respondents	81	92	78	69
All minority ethnic groups	77	90	73	66
Black African	86	93	86	79
Black Caribbean	80	91	79	71
Chinese	75	84	69	62
Indian	76	91	72	58
Pakistani	65	86	57	55
Bangladeshi	62	84	60	53
Mixed ethnic origin	85	90	78	81
Other	79	89	78	67

Base: all adults in employment
Source: *ONS Labour Force Survey, UK*, 2004

Participation in learning by terminal age of education

Terminal age of education is an important predictor of participation in learning as an adult, with a key divide existing between those who leave school at the earliest opportunity and those who stay on, even for a short while. Among the minority ethnic population, 58 per cent of those who left school as early as possible are learning, compared with just over 70 per cent of those who left full-time education aged 17–20, and 83 per cent of those who completed their education aged 21 and over (see Table 12).

The benefit of staying on in full-time education until at least 21, in terms of increased participation in learning, is greatest among Bangladeshi and Pakistani adults, although it is also higher than average for Chinese and Indian adults.

Table 12: Participation in learning by age completed full-time education, by ethnicity

	All who have completed full-time education %	Up to 16 %	17–18 %	19–20 %	21+ %
All respondents	78	68	81	83	90
All minority ethnic groups	72	58	71	73	83
Black African	80	70	81	79	85
Black Caribbean	77	71	81	76	87
Chinese	75	52	71	74	84
Indian	73	55	69	71	84
Pakistani	57	43	52	65	77
Bangladeshi	53	38	52	64	75
Mixed ethnic origin	79	69	79	86	89
Other	75	61	70	74	83

Base: all adults of working age who have completed full time education
Source: *ONS Labour Force Survey, UK*, 2004

Participation in learning by marital status

Among the general adult population, adults who are married or cohabiting (65 per cent) are more likely to be learning than those who are not (61 per cent). Among adults from minority ethnic groups as a whole, the opposite is true. 61 per cent of adults from minority ethnic groups who are married or cohabiting are learning compared with 68 per cent who are not.

People of Bangladeshi origin are distinctive in that they are the only group whose propensity to engage in learning goes up with marriage. The opposite is true for Chinese, Indian and Pakistani people, while marital status makes no difference to participation among other groups.

Table 13: Participation in learning by whether or not married/cohabiting, by ethnicity

	All %	Married or cohabiting %	Not married or cohabiting %
All respondents	64	65	61
All minority ethnic groups	63	61	68
African	77	77	77
Caribbean	65	64	65
Chinese	68	66	70
Indian	63	61	68
Pakistani	48	44	55
Bangladeshi	40	55	34
Mixed ethnic origin	76	76	76
Other	68	68	69

Base: all adults
Source: *ONS Labour Force Survey, UK*, 2004

Participation in learning by religion

Over two-thirds of Jews (76 per cent) Christians (73 per cent) Hindus (67 per cent), and adults who say that they have no religious affiliation report participation in learning, compared with jut over one half of Muslims (52 per cent) and Sikhs (56 per cent).

Given the role that learning can play in building understanding and respect for difference the significant under-representation of people with Muslim faith affiliation in learning is a serious challenge to education and training in public, private and informal provision.

Table 14: Participation in learning, by religion

	All %	All adults from minority ethnic groups %
Christian	62	73
Buddhist	73	65
Hindu	67	67
Jewish	72	76
Muslim	52	52
Sikh	56	56
Any other religion	69	66
No religion	72	70

Base: all adults

Source: *ONS Labour Force Survey, UK*, 2004